D0284931
FAIRY TALE BATTLE ROYALE
4

Contents

Chapter 13:
Emblem
003

Chapter 14:
Second Coming
043

Chapter 15:
Old Tales
081

Chapter 16:
Farewell
119

Chapter 17:
Contact
143

Chapter 13: Emblem

IT WOULD BE BETTER TO, IN CASE YOU NEED IT...
IF YOU DRINK THE CONTENTS OF THE WHITE RABBIT'S BOTTLE, YOU CAN GET *REALLY* BIG. IF YOU WAIT LONG ENOUGH, YOU CAN GET AS BIG AS THE CATERPILLAR.
IF YOU'D LIKE...
DON'T NEED IT.

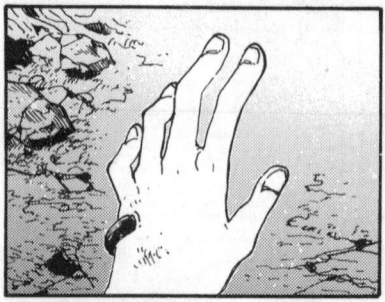

GASP

OH NO...
POP

ARE WE GOING THE RIGHT WAY?
AH!
YES!
WE ARE!
I WISH I'D HAD AN ITEM THAT WOULD MAKE US MOVE FASTER...
grip...
AKARI-CHAN!
Thanks! ♡♡
JUST BECAUSE YOU'RE INSIDE DOESN'T MEAN YOU CAN DRESS LIKE THAT! YOU'LL CATCH A COLD!
YEAH, YEAH...

YOU HEARD ME, DIDN'T YOU?
WHAT'S UP?
YOUR MOM AGAIN?
YEAH, YEAH! I GOT IT!
HELLO?
AND BESIDES, HAVEN'T YOU BEEN STAYING UP A LITTLE TOO LATE?
MOM...
I GET IT...
Calling
Tomo

BLAM PON! PON! PON! PON!
I'M SO HAPPY! THIS IS THE BEST!
LOVE YOU, AS USUAL...

BOFF
YOU WANTED TO GIVE HER THAT WHITE FLOWER BROOCH, RIGHT?
MORE IMPORTANTLY, IT'S MISAKI'S BIRTHDAY SOON, AND I WANNA TALK ABOUT HER PRESENT.
YOU SHOULD BE HAPPY SHE CARES ABOUT YOU. I'M SO JEALOUS.
I'D TRADE YOU, BUT NO TAKE-BACKS, YOU HEAR?
AHA HA!
KA-CHAK

A WHITE ROSE WOULD BE GREAT.
A WHITE ROSE BROOCH.
HM? A ROSE BROOCH?
THAT MIGHT BE A BIT TOO FLASHY, YOU KNOW?
NO WAY. IT'S PER-FECT!
THE FOUR OF US SHOULD GET MATCHING BROOCHES!
I WANT ONE, TOO!
I COULD GET MY FAVORITE...
A RED ROSE!

HM?
IT'S ACTUALLY SIX AREAS, INCLUDING MINE.
UNDERSTOOD.
THEY'RE NOT VERY LARGE, SO--
ABOUT FIVE MORE AREAS, AND WE SHOULD BE THERE!
AH...
YES!
HOW MUCH LONGER TO OUR DESTINATION?
I THINK YOU'LL BE OKAY. BUT JUST TO BE SURE, I'LL GIVE YOU THE SAFEST ROUTE POSSIBLE.
THERE'RE A WHOLE BUNCH OF PROTAGONISTS WHO LIVE THERE THAT I HAVEN'T MADE CONTACT WITH YET.
BUT THOSE AREAS...
f you know anything about this, will you tell me?
You're hiding something, aren't you?
Just tell me something, anything...
'm so scared.
ot rid of the ivy, then the mummies. In the end, everything vanished.
es that mean they're all dead?
so sick of your lip service.
hat the hell is this?
SOME OF THE PROTAGONISTS I'VE MET ARE PRETTY DANGEROUS, TOO.
I'M JUST BEING CAUTIOUS!
IS IT DANGEROUS?

EVERY-ONE'S STARTING TO FIGURE OUT THIS ISN'T A GAME, RIGHT?
CLICK
YOU DON'T HAVE ANY IVY GROWING ON YOU YET, DO YOU, KUNINAKA-SAN?
IF YOU DO, YOU SHOULD COME STRAIGHT TO MY AREA!
UNDER-STOOD. OKAY, WELL...
I'LL GET GOING.
ALSO!
IF YOU SEE ANY GROUPS OF PROTAGO-NISTS...
DON'T APPROACH THEM, IF YOU CAN HELP IT.
THAT'S...

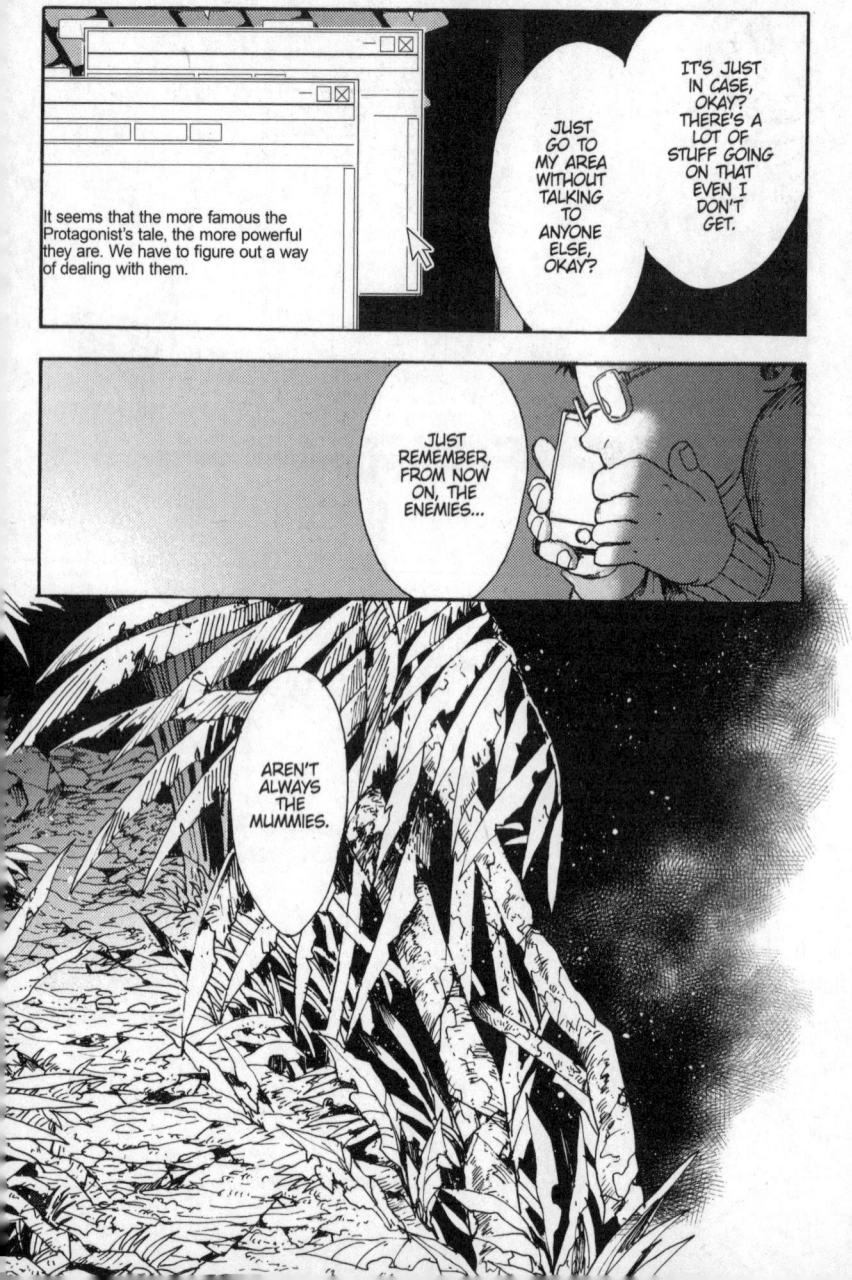
It seems that the more famous the Protagonist's tale, the more powerful they are. We have to figure out a way of dealing with them.
JUST GO TO MY AREA WITHOUT TALKING TO ANYONE ELSE, OKAY?
IT'S JUST IN CASE, OKAY? THERE'S A LOT OF STUFF GOING ON THAT EVEN I DON'T GET.
JUST REMEMBER, FROM NOW ON, THE ENEMIES...
AREN'T ALWAYS THE MUMMIES.

THE OTHER PROTAG-ONISTS ARE ENEMIES ...

RUSTLE
RUSTLE

"FROM NOW ON, EVERYONE WILL BE STEALING EVERYONE ELSE'S MUMMIES."

CHAK
GASP
AND WHEN I NEED TO GET RID OF THE IVY, I HAVE TO GO BACK TO MY OWN AREA...
EVERY MUMMY IN AN AREA MAY BE THE LAST ONE.
IT'S DIFFICULT TO SUSS OUT HOW MANY MAIN CAST PEOPLE THERE ARE.
DEPENDING ON THE FAIRY TALE, THE SIZE OF THE CAST CAN VARY WIDELY.

!!
ME.

SHOOT ME.

SLEEP NOW.

....!

ニヤリ
GLINT

BLAM
SNAP
SNAP
SNAP
WHAT ARE YOU--?
IT ISN'T RIGHT FOR US TO ATTACK THEM!
THE PROTAGONIST OF THIS AREA WILL...!
ドオ
UTHUUUUD

YOU'VE GOT IVY GROWING ON YOU, DON'T YOU, RED RIDING HOOD?
THEN WHY WOULD YOU...?!
BECAUSE THEY'RE NOT TOOLS FOR HEALING YOURSELF!
!
RED RIDING...
HOOD...
RUSTLE
RUSTLE
RUSTLE

!
RED RIDING HOOD!!
BAM

RUSTLE...
A...
ARE YOU OKAY?!
!
THUD
SLINK
SLINK
WELL?
HOW DID IT GO?
THAT GIRL WAS RED RIDING HOOD.
DANG.
RED RIDING HOOD...!
AND THE OTHER ONE...
LOOKS LIKE... ALICE...?

WHISPER
HER BOOK.
GET IT!
WHISPER
!
MURMUR
I-I'M...
.....
I'M SORRY SHE SHOT YOU!
GLARE...
RUSTLE
GLARE
.....
SHE WAS JUST STARTLED BY YOUR SHADOWS.
WE'RE NOT GONNA TOUCH YOUR MAIN CAST!
YOUR BOOK, PLEASE.

HUH?

GIVE US YOUR BOOK AND NO ONE GETS HURT.

STARE...
WE THINK IT'S UNFAIR.

MY BOOK...?
I CAN'T.
HOW WOULD I GET HOME?

STARE
WE'VE STUMBLED ACROSS FAMOUS PROTAGO-NISTS BEFORE.
THE MORE FAMOUS YOUR FAIRY TALE, THE MORE POWERFUL YOU BECOME.
YOU'RE A DANGER TO US.

THE STRONG ALWAYS WISH TO RULE OVER THE WEAK.
BUT BEFORE THAT...
Chak
WE NEED TO RUN!!
DASH
RUSTLE
RUSTLE

FU...
FUKUSHIGE-SAN TOLD ME...
TO BE CAREFUL OF LARGE GROUPS!
LET ME...
THIS...!
THIS IS WHAT HE MEANT!
HUH?!
CRASH

HUH...?

GOT 'EM!
NICE.
WE DID IT!
HURRY! SHUT 'EM IN!

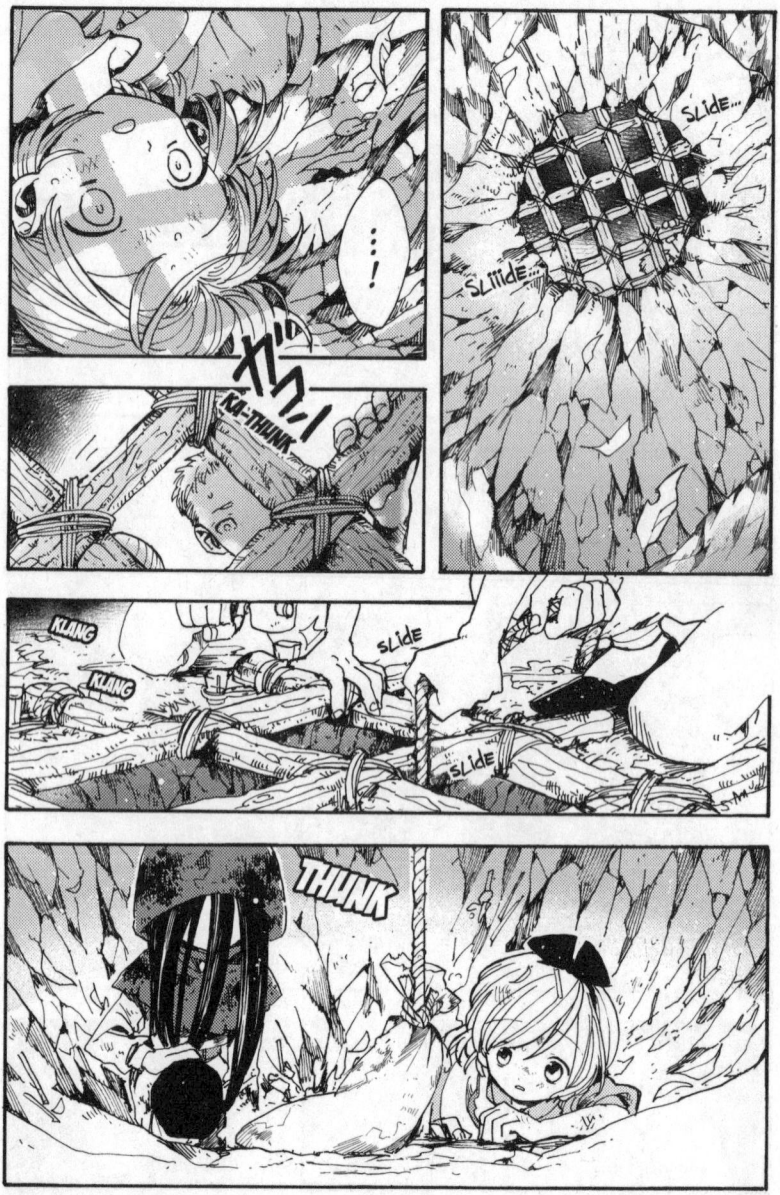
……!
ガクッ!
KA-THUNK
SLIDE...
SLIIIDE...
KLANG
KLANG
SLIDE
SLIDE
THUNK

GLARE
IF YOU DON'T, WE'LL JUST LEAVE YOU TO THE IVY.
...!
PUT YOUR BOOKS INTO THAT BAG.
AS SOON AS WE GET THEM, WE'LL LET YOU OUT.

I'M SORRY...
PLINK

I'M...

HUH?
WHAT?!
AH...!

p://twitter.com/Noah!!.
Noah!!
GO HOME?!
WHAT ABOUT YOU, RED...?
YOU SHOULD GO HOME.
FWIP
THAT'S MY...!
WAIT...!
COME BACK IN A LITTLE WHILE.
BUT THIS...
IT'S MY...!
YOU'RE IN MY WAY.

WAIT!
RED RIDING HOOD!
AH...!
SHF
SHF
OW!
OWW...

BANG
AOBA ?!!
JOLT
!!

BAM
RED RIDING HOOD!

B...
BIG SISTER!
WHERE WERE YOU JUST NOW?!
AND HOW DID YOU GET HOME SO QUICK?!

AH...!

SNATCH

I'M SORRY ...
I'LL TELL YOU ALL ABOUT IT LATER.

YOU'VE BEEN ACTING REALLY WEIRD...
AND I CAN'T KEEP TURNING A BLIND EYE!
...!

NOT LATER! WE'RE TALKING ABOUT THIS NOW!

...!
ONE OF THEM WENT HOME.
IT'S COOL.
WE'LL WATCH FOR THEM.

LET'S CATCH MORE AND MORE OF THESE FAMOUS PROTAGONISTS!
TO GIVE OURSELVES A FAIR SHOT!

IF HER IVY GROWS, SHE'LL HAND HER BOOK OVER.
KER-CHAK

SLAM
TMP
IT'S...
IT'S OKAY!
WE KNEW HER WEAPONS MIGHT BE THIS STRONG!
GO GET ANOTHER COVER FOR THE TRAP!
KRNCH
KRNCH

GLINT
BLAM
SHE'S WIDENING THE ENTRANCE!
BLAM
QUICK! CLOSE THE--
WHOA!
IT'S TIME FOR YOU TO EXPLAIN YOURSELF!
BIG SISTER ...
BUT...!
AOBA!
BLAAAM
KER-CHAK

PLEASE GIVE ME MY BOOK...!
...?!
WHAT IS WRONG WITH YOU?!
HOW MANY DAYS OF SCHOOL HAVE YOU MISSED?!
YOUR TEACHER WAS SO WORRIED THAT HE CAME TO CHECK UP ON YOU.
whisper whisper
AH...
PARDON ME FOR ELBOWING MY WAY IN...
KAWADA-SENSEI?!
OH NO...
WHY DID I...
OH!
PLEASE DON'T TROUBLE YOURSELF.

SNATCH
HEY!
I'M JUST GLAD YOU'RE SAFE.
I'M SORRY. I HAVEN'T BEEN HERE MUCH...
REALLY, IT'S NOT A PROBLEM.
AOBA !!
I'M SORRY, BIG I...! SISTER ...
DIDN'T I JUST TELL YOU THAT THIS IS NO TIME FOR READING?!
YOU'RE COMING WITH ME TO HAVE A LITTLE TALK!
AH...
NOW, NOW, WAKABA-SAN...
I JUST CAME OVER TO MAKE SURE THAT AOBA WAS OKAY.

TEACH-ER...
DO YOU FEEL UP TO GOING BACK TO SCHOOL, KUNINAKA-SAN?

IT'S GETTING LATE.
WE'LL TALK SOON, OKAY?

ONCE YOU FEEL LIKE YOU CAN HANDLE IT, THAT IS.
DON'T YOU THINK?

THE SOONER YOU COME BACK, THE BETTER...

I...
UNDER-STAND...

DON'T PUSH YOURSELF TOO HARD.

THE SOONER THE BETTER.

THANK YOU, WAKABA-SAN...
I MUST TAKE MY LEAVE.
AH...
ALREADY?
I'M SO SORRY, WE HAVEN'T SHOWN YOU ANY HOSPITALITY AT ALL...
NO, IT'S FINE. I JUST CAME TO SEE HER.

AOBA!
I'M GOING TO GO SEE HIM TO THE DOOR. YOU BETTER NOT MOVE!
I'LL BE BACK SOON, YOU HEAR ME?!

SLAM
I'M SORRY...
SISTER.

THANK YOU FOR COMING.
THANK YOU.
AND PLEASE PARDON MY INTRUSION.
AOBA, YOUR TEACHER'S GONE.
COME DOWNSTAIRS SO WE CAN TALK.
TMP
TMP
WHAA-AAAT ?!
Sorry, Big Sister. I'll be back soon.
AOBA ?!
ガチャ
KER-CHAK
...
YOU'RE KIDDING...

RUSTLE...
WHY...
ARE YOU...
I DON'T CARE ABOUT YOU.
I SIMPLY...
WISH TO PASS THROUGH.
SPLASH
HOW...
CAN YOU EVEN MOVE...?

CRASH
AHHH?!
WHAT...?
CLATTER
CLATTER

WHAT HAP-PENED ...?

CLATTER

CREAK-CREAK

JUST A LITTLE...
MORE...!

CLACK
CREAK
HUFF... HUFF...
HUUUUFF !!

CREAK

HUH...?
LET'S GO.
KAWADA

I'M HOME.
AH, IT'S DADDY!
DADDY!!
RATTLE...

KER-chak.

IT'S OKAY.
YOU MUST BE TIRED.

SAYURI!
YOUR FATHER'S HOME!
MM-HMM...

WELCOME HOME, DEAR.
AH...
SORRY I'M LATE.

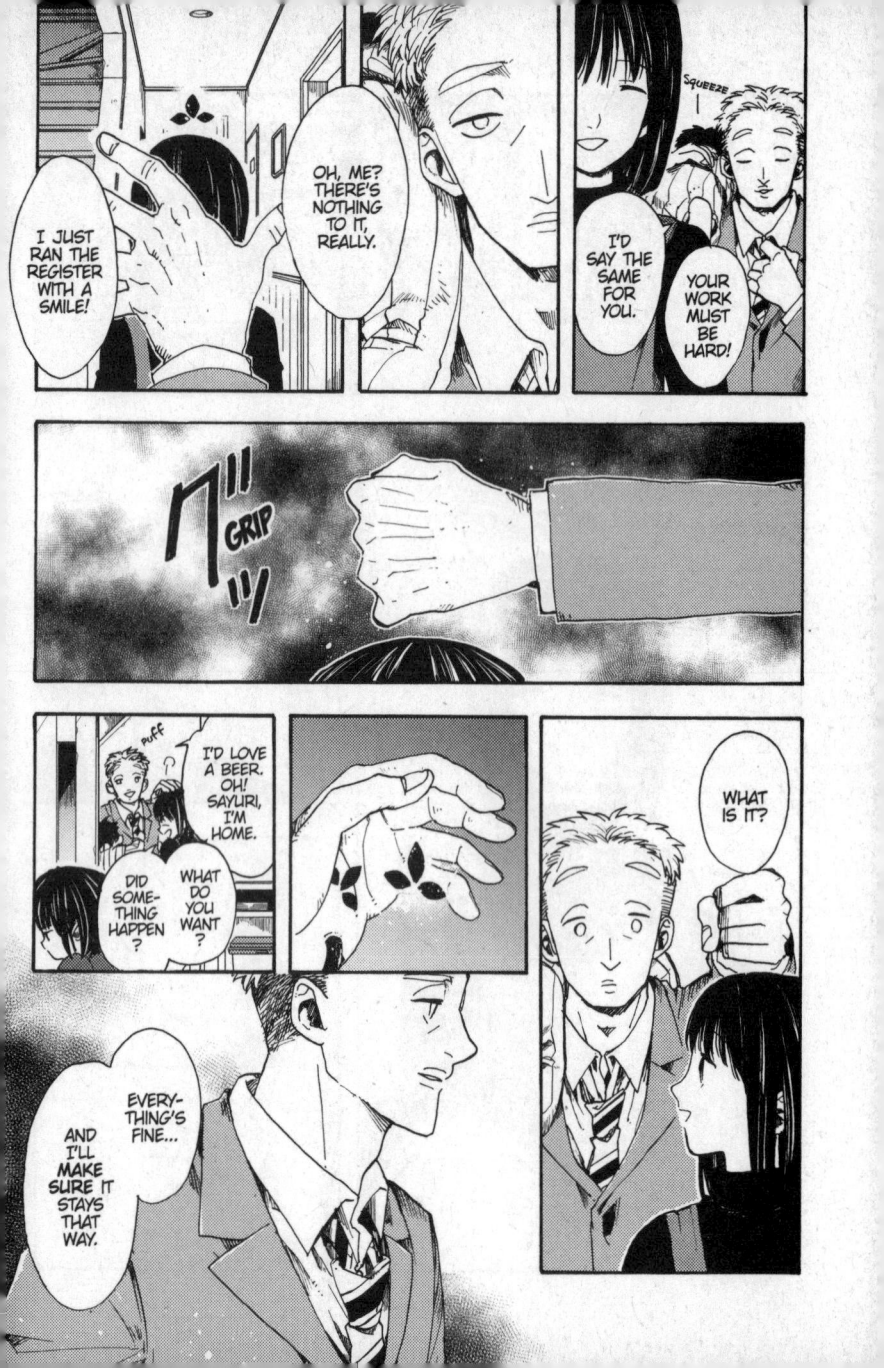
I JUST RAN THE REGISTER WITH A SMILE!
OH, ME? THERE'S NOTHING TO IT, REALLY.
SQUEEZE
I'D SAY THE SAME FOR YOU.
YOUR WORK MUST BE HARD!
GRIP
PUFF
I'D LOVE A BEER. OH! SAYURI, I'M HOME.
DID SOME-THING HAPPEN ?
WHAT DO YOU WANT ?
WHAT IS IT?
EVERY-THING'S FINE...
AND I'LL MAKE SURE IT STAYS THAT WAY.

FAIRY
TALE
BATTLE
ROYALE

FAIRY TALE BATTLE ROYALE

Chapter 14: Second Coming

RUSTLE...

RUSTLE
RUSTLE
RED RIDING HOOD...

RUSTLE...
RUSTLE...

THOSE PEOPLE WHO TRAPPED US MIGHT FIND US AGAIN...
SO SHOULDN'T WE TAKE ANOTHER ROUTE?

RUSTLE
!
RUSTLE
RUSTLE
RUSTLE
STAY THERE.
CLINT
BLOCK
LET'S GO.
MOVE.

!
I DIDN'T KILL THEM.
NO ONE KNOWS ABOUT THE PROTAG-ONISTS HERE, ANYWAY.
WE SHOULD JUST LEAVE.
IF YOU FIRE YOUR GUN...
THEY'LL HEAR US.
THEY WON'T.
IF WE RETURN TO YOUR AREA, THEN I'LL BE IN A BIND.
WHEN YOU...
SAY IT LIKE THAT...!
ARE YOU OKAY?
WE BETTER GET THOSE WOUNDS LOOKED AT.

WE CAN'T DO ANYTHING.
IT'S ALMOST LIKE...
...
IT'S UNFAIR THAT THE FAMOUS ONES HAVE SUCH AN ADVANTAGE.
I KNEW SHE'D BE STRONG, BUT I DIDN'T EXPECT HER TO BE IMMORTAL ...
WHAT KIND OF STORY IS THAT ITEM EVEN FROM?!

THAT'S TRUE.
MIGHT AS WELL...
THERE MAY BE NEW INFO ON THE INTERNET BY NOW.
WE NEED TIME TO REGROUP.
ANYONE THAT'S TIRED OR INJURED CAN GO HOME.

RUSTLE

IS THAT A MUMMY?
NO, DEFINITELY NOT.
RUSTLE
WE'RE HAVING A LOT OF VISITORS.
LEAVE MY AREA IMMEDIATELY!
I DON'T MIND TALKING TO YOU, BUT GIVE ME YOUR BOOK FIRST!
CREAK
I-IT HURTS...
MUMBLE
MUST ... HUNT ...
MUMBLE

"KILL ME..."
...!
BECAUSE I WAS TOLD TO KILL THEM.
WHY DID YOU DO THAT...?
THUD
BUT STILL ...!
RUSTLE
!

THAT'S THE SAME LIGHT THAT SHONE WHEN NOAH DISAP-PEARED...
RUMBLE...
RUMBLE
RUMBLE
RUMBLE
RUMBLE
SLIP...
RUMBLE...
RUMBLE...
RUMBLE...

CREEEEEEEEEAK
RUMBLE
RUMBLE
RUMBLE
RUMBLE
RUMBLE
DASHI!
RUMBLE
RUMBLE
THE PROTAGONIST OF THIS AREA HAS GONE.
WE HAVE TO GET OUT BEFORE WE DISAPPEAR ALONG WITH IT.
RUMBLE
RUMBLE

AH...
AH... AH...
DASH
RUMBLE...
I'M SORRY.
RUMBLE
RUMBLE
WHY DIDN'T SHE KILL ME?
RUMBLE
SLIDE...
RUMBLE...
RUMBLE

BUT...
IT HAPPENS TO THEIR MAIN CAST, TOO...?
SQUEEZE
SLIDE
SLIDE
SLIDE
SLIDE
I WONDER HOW MANY PROTAG-ONISTS I'VE SEEN DISAPPEAR.
RUMBLE
IT'S JUST LIKE RED RIDING HOOD SAID. IF NOAH IS STILL IN THE STORY WORLD...
RUMBLE
BEFORE AN AREA DISAPPEARS, THE MUMMIES GET COVERED IN IVY, TOO!
RUMBLE
WOULDN'T HE BE WITH HIS MAIN CAST...?
HUFF ...
HUFF ...

5:00 RUMBLE...
5:00 RUMBLE
5:00 RUMBLE

"MAYBE WE CAN GET OUT A LITTLE QUICKER."
"IT'S SO COLD!!"
WHOOSH
HUFF...
SHIVER...
HUFF...

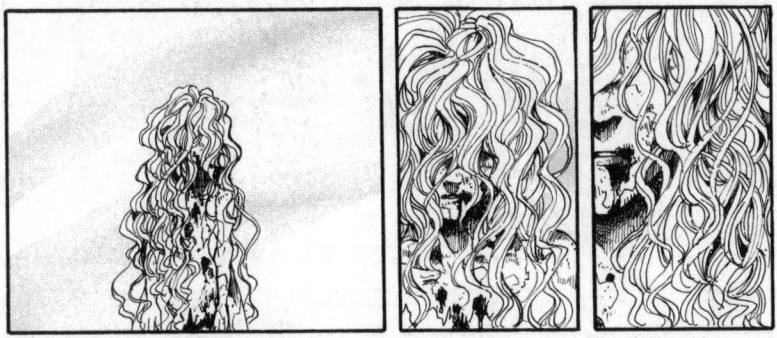

I WANT TO GO HOME ...

PLOD...
PLOD...

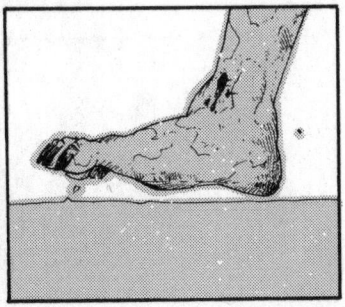

JUST LIKE BEFORE ...

YES, WE'RE HERE. IT'S JUST AS FUKUSHIGE-SAN DESCRIBED.
FWIP

shake
shake

SO, ARE WE IN THE NEXT AREA?
GASP
I'M ...
I'M SORRY!

RED RIDING HOOD...
UM...

DO YOU KNOW WHY THAT AREA'S MAIN CAST WAS COVERED IN IVY?
AND...

WE SHOULD KEEP GOING.

YOU MEAN... A PROTAG-ONIST KILLED ...?
OR...
AND BECAUSE SHE WAS SUPPOSED TO KILL THEM AND DIDN'T, HER MAIN CAST GOT COVERED IN IVY.
BECAUSE ANOTHER PROTAGONIST KILLED HER, SO HER AREA DISAPPEARED.
!
IF THAT PROTAGONIST STILL HAD A MAIN CAST, WHY DID SHE...
...
SHE WISHED FOR IT.
——!
HOW CAN YOU BE SO CALM ABOUT THIS?!
PEOPLE ARE DYING...!
THEY AREN'T DEAD. THEY'RE JUST NOT IN THE STORY WORLD.
THAT'S NOT WHAT I MEANT!

THAT MAY BE TRUE, BUT WE REALLY DON'T HAVE ANY ANSWERS, DO WE?! SO WHY ...?!
GASP

I'M SORRY ...
I...
"LET'S TAKE A BREAK!
"SINCE WE MANAGED TO RENEW THIS TOWN!"

IF WE KNOW WHERE WE'RE GOING, WE SHOULD KEEP...
UM!
RED RIDING HOOD!
WHY ...
WHY DON'T WE TAKE A BREAK ?!
....?

Squeeeeeze
A...
A LOT HAS HAPPENED. LET'S HAVE SOME TEA...
A-AND TALK IT OVER.
...
N...
I'M REALLY TIRED.
NO, WAIT! I MEAN, I...
M...
ME AND YOU, WE'RE...
WHY?

IF YOU'D LIKE TO, THAT IS...
BUT ONLY...

I'VE HAD TEA THERE ONCE BEFORE...
TURN

HOW ABOUT THAT BUILDING? IT LOOKS LIKE IT'S BEEN RE-FRESHED RECENTLY!
OH!
!

WHERE?
GLOOOW

TEA...
TMP TMP
YOU JUST WAIT HERE, OKAY?
I'LL MAKE SOME TEA.
SILENCE
PHEW!
SNIFF...
PLINK...
CREAK
MAYBE IT'S IN THIS CAN...?
UM... TO START A FIRE, I NEED...
I SHOULD'VE HELPED HIM.
WHEN NOAH-SAN MADE TEA BEFORE...
IT'S ...
IT'S PROBABLY OKAY. IT TASTED JUST FINE BEFORE!
I HAVE TO BOIL SOME WATER...
AH!
THAT'S RIGHT! I NEED MATCHES!
THERE SHOULD BE SOME LEFT IN HERE...
AFTER ALL, WE'RE IN THE LITTLE MATCH GIRL'S AREA...
RATTLE

CRASH
CLANG
カラーン

WE WON'T HURT YOU...!
!
WAIT, PLEASE!

WHERE ARE YOU GOING?
DASH

BANG
...!

BANG..

THAT GIRL IS COVERED IN IVY...
AND SHE MAY NOT KNOW HOW TO GET RID OF IT!

WAIT, PLEASE!
DASH
!
!
IF YOU STAY THIS WAY, YOU'LL...!

トー
TMP

I'M... HOME?
BUT HOW...?
HUH...?
DING
DONG
HUH? MY BOOK...
DID I USE MY BOOKMARK?
?
DING
DONG
YES ...
COMING!
EXCUSE M--
KER-CHAK

NOAH-SAN...?

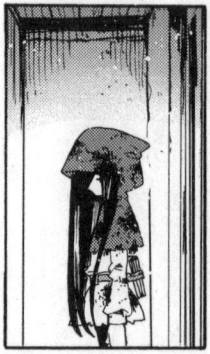

AOBA!

.....
CREEEAK
IF YOU PLAN ON STAYING, I'LL BE ON MY WAY.
SO TELL ME HOW--

WHAT ARE YOU...?
!
……
ポッ
PFF
CLACK
ニャッ
RUSTLE
!
KA-CHAK

I REALLY WANTED YOU TO SEE IT. I GOT YOU SOME SWEET TICKETS!
OH, I'M SO HAPPY. WE CAN MAKE IT TO THE CONCERT IN TIME!

HERE'S YOUR VIP PASS!
TA-DA!

THAT'S AMAZING! YOU CAUGHT ON REAL QUICK!
NO...
I CAN'T TAKE CREDIT. I JUST WENT WHERE FUKUSHIGE-SAN TOLD ME.
RUSTLE...

I'M BACK IN THE PLACE WHERE WE HAD TEA...
IN THE LITTLE MATCH GIRL'S AREA.

WHAT'S UP, AOBA?

IT'S JUST AROUND THIS CORNER!
NOAH-SAN...
PAUSE

AND WHEN I DO, I PROMISE I'LL COME RUNNING!
BUT SOON, I'LL BE SOMEWHERE I CAN ASK ABOUT YOU.
THIS MUST BE SOMETHING I'VE DREAMED UP...
RIGHT BEFORE WE MET, I LOOKED INTO THE LITTLE MATCH GIRL'S FLAME.
TMP
I'LL DO MY BEST!
I'LL FIND YOU, NOAH-SAN, AND EVERYONE ELSE! AND THEN I'LL SAVE YOU ALL!

WE'LL SEE EACH OTHER AGAIN...
YES! WE WILL!
FZZZ
!!

JOLT
TMP
....!
RED RIDING HOOD!
WHY?! MY FLAMES SHOULDN'T GO OUT SO EASILY...!
SLIDE
IT'S OKAY. I WON'T HURT YOU. PLEASE...
PLEASE, LISTEN...!
JOMP
!!

I WANT TO SAVE YOU!
!
...?
I'M... BACK AT THE ORPHAN-AGE?
YAAAY!
HA HA HA!

CLATTER
!

GASP

BIG SISTER...

JOLT
BAM
WAIT!

AH, YOU SCARED ME!

WHAT'S WRONG ?

DON'T GO!
PUMP

AH...!
INSTEAD, I MADE MY OWN CONTRACT TO LOOK FOR YOU...!
WE SHOULD HAVE BEEN TOGETHER!
AND THAT WE DIDN'T MAKE A CONTRACT TOGETHER!
I'VE ALWAYS REGRETTED NOT STOPPING YOU THAT DAY...
IF YOU GO THERE, YOU WON'T COME HOME AGAIN.

RED RIDING HOOD!

WOW
!

GRIP

RUSTLE
Tmp
I...
I DON'T THINK SHE MEANT TO HURT US!

AH...

SHE WAS JUST PROTECTING HERSELF.
...?
I- I'M...
I'M SORRY...
I...
I...
DROPPED MY BOOK.
WHAT?
SERIOUSLY?!

FINALLY, SOME INFO!
MAN, KUNINAKA AND HER PARTY!
THEY'RE SUCH SOFTIES! SHE'S SAVING ME SO MUCH WORK!
HMM, AN AREA WITH A LARGE MOUNTAIN, NEAR A PURE WHITE AREA...
AH!
Subject: About the person you're looking for
Webmaster:
I have some information regarding the person you're looking for.
I saw them from an Area with a large mountain, in a nearby Area with a facade.
Can we meet up to talk about it?
THE ONLY AREA I DIDN'T KNOW THE NAME OF...
TAP
POP
Central Police Station
Subject: Definitely!
I look forward to talking with you!
How about you meet me at the Central Station Cafe tomorrow at 10AM?
AFTER THAT, I'VE GOTTA FIGURE OUT HOW TO GET RED RIDING HOOD ALONE...
THAT SEEMS LEGIT!
IT'S WORTH CHECKING OUT! GREAT!

WE'RE MEETING TOMORROW.
I GOT HIM.
IT'S MOMOSE.
Subject: RE: Definitely!
Understood.
I look forward to meeting with you.
CLICK
CLICK
CLACK
CLACK
WE HAVE TO FOLLOW JAPANESE LAW.
PLEASE JUST DON'T GO CRAZY ON THE GUY, OKAY?
I GOT IT...
AND KEEP IT DOWN!
AIMING FOR ZERO
WELL...
WHAAAAT?
If you see these faces, call 110 immediately!
Traffic Division
YEP, TOMORROW AT TEN AM.
HUH?
HE'S REALLY COMING?
Tokyo Metropolitan Police
OKAY, TEN AM IT IS, THEN.
Is there a ringleader?
→ Government ○
→ Business ×
→ Protagonist △
→ Webmaster △
Person we're looking for
Wolf Woman
☆ The Protagonist killing other Protagonists
↳ Can become a woman, mummy, or beast

FAIRY TALE BATTLE ROYALE

Chapter 15: Old Tales

I'M JUST GLAD I COULD HELP.
LOOM...
THANK YOU SO MUCH.
I CAN'T BELIEVE YOU GOT SO BIG...
DID YOU JUST EAT A MUSH-ROOM?
YES!
IT'S ONE OF ALICE'S ITEMS, AFTER ALL...
AND IF I EAT THE STALK, I CAN SHRINK BACK DOWN AGAIN.
OH, RIGHT!
GO AHEAD!
Gathering her book

I THINK HER MATCHES...
SHOW PEOPLE THEIR DEEPEST DESIRES.
WHEN I STRUCK A MATCH THAT FIRST TIME...
HER WISH TO HAVE NOAH COME TO HER HOUSE AND GIVE HER VIP TICKETS FOR HIS BAND.
IT WAS THE SAME WITH ME.
UM, I ABSOLUTELY DIDN'T SEE ANYTHING TOO AWFUL, SO PLEASE JUST FORGET IT...
THAT'S WHY...

BUT...

I SAW A FRIEND WHO'D MOVED AWAY.
I WAS SO HAPPY.

THANKS SO MUCH!

I'M OKAY FOR NOW!
I'LL GO ON AHEAD AND LIGHT THE FIRE!

WHY DON'T YOU BOTH COME OVER TO MY PLACE AND TAKE A BREAK?
YOU PREPARED SOME TEA, DIDN'T YOU?
!
WE SHOULD GET RID OF YOUR IVY FIRST.

WILL YOU COME INSIDE WITH ME?

WE'RE MAKING SOME TEA.
WHEN IT'S READY WE'LL CALL YOU.

...

IF YOU'D ONLY TALKED TO US...
YOU WERE HIDING HERE WHEN NOAH AND I CAME BEFORE?

WHAAAT ?!

I'M SORRY I DIDN'T STOP HER...

BUT RED RIDING HOOD ISN'T A BAD PER--
OH, IT'S ALL RIGHT.

I THOUGHT ABOUT IT... BUT I GOT SCARED BY THOSE GUNSHOTS.
UGH...
TH-THAT'S RIGHT, I RE-MEMBER.
?
?

THERE'S ...
ALL SORTS OF FOLKS HERE.
A...
AOBA-SAN!
AT LAST, I THOUGHT I COULD FINALLY...
SEE HER AGAIN.
WHERE ARE YOU...?

BIG SISTER...
YOU'RE ALREADY...
I GUESS...
JOLT!
POP

...
KA
SHAK
WHY...?
WHY?
WHY IS IT ONLY...
YOU?
TMP...
NO...

I JUST WANTED TO SEE YOU AGAIN.

SISTER, NO...
I...

COME INSIDE.

GRIP

HERE YOU ARE.

BUT...
IF WE RUN, SHE WON'T CATCH US.
SHE FOLLOWED YOU HERE.
YOUR BIG SISTER...?
ARE YOU SEARCHING FOR...
UM...
RED RIDING HOOD...
I...
I HAVE AN OLDER SISTER, TOO.
TWITCH
SHE'S QUITE A BIT OLDER.
MORE LIKE MY MOM.

OUR PARENTS ARE DOCTORS, SO THEY'RE ALMOST NEVER HOME.

WHEN SHE SAW ME PLAYING ALONE, SHE'D TAKE ME OUTSIDE. WE PLAYED OUR HEARTS OUT.
WHEN I WAS LITTLE, I WAS SCARED TO SLEEP ALONE. SO SHE'D SLEEP NEXT TO ME.

SHE USED TO READ TO ME.
THAT'S WHY I LOVE FAIRY TALES.

WHAT IS *YOUR* SISTER LIKE?

...

AH!
HER CONTRACTED FAIRY TALE IS "THE WEREWOLF'S DAUGHTER," RIGHT?
THERE ARE STILL SO MANY STORIES I DON'T KNOW.

I'LL ...
I'LL GO PUT ON SOME MORE TEA.
LOOKS LIKE THE POT GOT COLD.
I'LL ...
COME HELP.
"THE WERE-WOLF'S DAUGHTER" ...

REALLY? I GUESS THINGS CHANGE ...
FROM COUNTRY TO COUNTRY, HUH?
NO...

IT USED TO BE THE MOST WELL-KNOWN STORY IN THE WORLD.
THAT'S WHAT MY SISTER TOLD ME.

WAS A VERY FAMOUS FAIRY TALE.

JUST LIKE AESOP'S FABLES...
OR GRIMM'S FAIRY TALES...
UNTIL ABOUT ONE HUNDRED YEARS AGO.
YES.
WHAT? YOU MEAN ONE HUNDRED YEARS...
I...
BEFORE ...
YOU SAID IT'S 2016, YES?

I...
I SIGNED MY CONTRACT...
IN 1916.
EXACTLY ONE HUNDRED YEARS AGO.
1916.
WAAA-AAH!!

MAT-THEW'S HOGGING THE BALL!
NOOOO! THAT'S NOT TRUE! I WAS ABOUT TO GIVE HIM A TURN!
GOODNESS, WHAT'S ALL THIS FUSS ABOUT?
MONIKA!
BIG SISTER!

MONIKA THE GREAT HAS STOLEN THE BALL!

SNATCH!
HEY!

YOU'RE LYING! YOU WERE NEVER GONNA GIVE ME THE BALL!
ANYWAY, YOU ALWAYS HOG THE ART SUPPLIES!

YEAH !!
LET'S GO GET THE BALL, CLAIRE!

COME AND GET IT!
AH!!
DASH

Mitä on annettu
Yksi toive
sijasta
Little Red Riding Hood
Punahenkilö:
Little Red Riding Hood

COME LOOK...
I FOUND THIS ON MY DESK.
SO, YOU GOT ONE, TOO?
"CONTRACT" ...
AND IT HAS MY NAME ON IT?
AH...
IS THAT FOR YOU?
sopimus
Mitä on annettu
Yksi toive
sijasta
Miss.Monika
sopimus
Mitä on annettu
Yksi toive
sijasta
Päähenkilö:
The Werewolf's Daughter
HUH?
WHERE DID THEY GET SUCH GOOD PAPER?
I HAVE A FEELING THAT MATTHEW OR LIZA IS BEHIND THIS.
IT'S A VERY THOROUGH LITTLE PRANK...
WELL, NOW...
HOW AMAZING TO HAVE A CONTRACT FOR SUCH A FAMOUS FAIRY TALE!
A WISH...
MINE'S "LITTLE RED RIDING HOOD."
OH, THIS PART'S DIFFERENT... LOOK.
MY FAIRY TALE IS "THE WEREWOLF'S DAUGHTER."

DON'T BE SILLY.
MAYBE YOU SHOULD WISH TO ELOPE WITH YOUR BOY-FRIEND.

I'LL NEVER LEAVE THIS ORPHANAGE.
I'D RATHER WISH FOR THIS ROOF TO FINALLY GET REPLACED.
BUT, MONIKA, YOU'RE GROWN-UP.
I'LL TAKE YOUR PLACE.

THAT'S TRUE. YOU HAVEN'T CALLED ME "BIG SISTER" IN A WHILE.
SST...
WELL, IT'S NOT LIKE WE'RE RELATED BY BLOOD, RIGHT?

CLAMOR
WHOA, REALLY?!
THIS PLACE?
REBUILT?

HEE HEE! OH, CHILD ...
WE RENTED SOME ROOMS IN THE ORPHANAGE IN THE NEXT TOWN.
WHERE? A HOTEL?! WHERE?
SISTER...

YES. CON-STRUCTION WILL BEGIN NEXT MONTH.
WE'VE MANAGED TO SECURE TEMPORARY HOUSING AS WELL.

WHICH IS SUCH A SHAME. I WANTED TO THANK THEM.
THEY DIDN'T LEAVE THEIR NAME, JUST THE FUNDS WE NEEDED ...
SOME KIND-HEARTED SOUL MADE A DONATION.

OH, ABOUT THAT...
BUT HOW CAN YOU AFFORD IT? WE'RE IN THE MIDDLE OF A REVOLUTION.

HEY, WILL MY ROOM BE RENOVATED, TOO?
EVEN THOUGH...
IT WAS SO DARK, WHEN I OPENED MY EYES...
I WAS IN THE WORLD OF "THE WEREWOLF'S DAUGHTER"!
OKAY, SIS...
YOU DON'T BELIEVE ME, DO YOU?
IT'S IMPOSSIBLE.
AND THE RENOVATION'S JUST A COINCIDENCE.
OHO HO HO! I KNEW YOU'D SAY THAT.
BEHOLD!
THE SYMBOL IS PROOF!
TA-DA!

10/ 15
10/ 16
10/ 10
ARE YOU KIDDING ME?!
AM I THE ONLY ONE WHO CAN SEE IT?!
THE NOT TH
OKAY!
glance
glance
LET'S ALL MAKE SURE TO GATHER UP ALL OUR BELONGINGS, OKAY?
OKAY, EVERYONE! TOMORROW WE MOVE INTO OUR TEMPORARY QUARTERS!
SISTER, HAVE YOU SEEN MONIKA?
MO-NIKA?
I JUST SAW HER IN THE KITCHEN.

MONIKA? ARE YOU THERE?
AH...
WHAT ARE YOU DOING?!
SNATCH
ガッ
I'M... JUST TRYING TO...
CUT OFF THE IVY.

NO, I HAV-EN'T...
DON'T YOU DARE SIGN THAT CON-TRACT!
THROW IT AWAY!
I'M BEGGING YOU!
...?!
HEY...
YOU HAVEN'T SIGNED IT, HAVE YOU?!
WHAT HAPPENED TO YOUR CONTRACT?
TUG
WHAT?
WHAT WAS THAT?
...!
GRIND
THANK GOD...
THANK GOD...!
I... BURNED THEM OFF.

WHY ARE YOU ACTING LIKE THIS?!
TWITCH
...!
MONIKA!
THAT'S NOT GOOD!
...!
SWAY...
WHAT HAP-PENED TO YOU?!
YOU'RE ALWAYS KEEPING EVERYTHING TO YOUR-SELF!
YOU THINK I'M A CHILD, DON'T YOU?!
I NEVER ASKED FOR THAT! IT EATS ME UP INSIDE!
I'M SORRY...

HERE YOU GO.
IT'S HEAVY.
THANKS!
MO---
Dash
MONIKA ...!
KER-CHAK
.....

SISTER...
WHERE'S MONIKA?
THE POLICE ARE SEARCHING FOR HER NOW.
LET US PRAY, AND WAIT.

WHERE ARE YOU GOING ?!
WAIT!
SPRINT

SISTER...
THE ORPHANAGE HASN'T BEEN TORN DOWN YET, RIGHT?
?
THAT'S RIGHT. IT'S TO-MOR-ROW.
WHEN BIG SISTER CAME HOME LAST TIME, DID SHE KNOW WHERE SHE WAS?

HUFF!
HUFF!

ゴロ ゴロ...
RUMBLE
RUMBLE...

RUSTLE
!

RUSTLE
RUSTLE
RUSTLE

ハアハア
HUFF...
HUFF...
sopimus
Mitä on annettu
Yksi toive
sijasta
Little Red Riding Hood
Päähenkilö:
Little Red Riding Hood

LET ME FIND HER ...!
PLEASE...
THEN...
WHAT HAP-PENED...?
YOU WENT THROUGH A LOT OF BAD THINGS TOO, RIGHT?
THEN?

ONE HUNDRED YEARS...
YOU'VE BEEN HERE FOR ONE HUNDRED YEARS?
YOU'VE BEEN A PROTAG-ONIST ALL THAT TIME?
THE MAIN CAST THAT DRIED UP AND BLEW AWAY.
THE WORLD THAT FED ON THEIR MURDERS.
THE ALICE THAT TURNED TO SAND.
THE WHITE BOOK.
AND I HAVEN'T EVEN BEEN HERE A MONTH.
.....
YES.
SO...
ALL OF THE PEOPLE IN HERE...
...?
.....
HERE IN THE STORY WORLD.

INCLUDING YOU.

YOU'VE MET THEM.

IF...
IF THAT'S THE CASE...
THE OTHER PROTAG-ONISTS THAT WERE HERE BEFORE...

WHAT ...?
YOU MEAN, WHEN I FIRST CAME HERE...
AND I MET...
THAT PERSON...

TH...
THAT...
ALICE...
WAS...
AH...!
!

TINK
YOU HAVE TO GET RID OF IT!
NO...
IT DOESN'T MATTER.
UM ...
YOU SEE, MY AREA'S BEEN REVIVED.
...!
SHIP...
KATJA-SAN...!
YOUR IVY!
SO THE IVY WOULD JUST COME BACK.
...!
I'LL TELL YOU WHERE THEY ARE. WHY DON'T YOU GO THERE?
AFTER WE'RE DONE, I'LL BE RIGHT BEHIND YOU.
IT WASN'T JUST PROTAG-ONISTS, YOU KNOW.
KATJA-SAN...
THERE'S LOTS OF PLACES IN MY AREA THAT HAVEN'T BEEN REVIVED.
TWITCH

THE OTHER REASON I KILLED PEOPLE...
WAS BECAUSE I WANTED TO GIVE THEM PEACE.
YOU HAVE AN EMBLEM.
AS DOES YOUR SUCCESSOR.
YOUR FAMILY AND FRIENDS BEAR IT, TOO.

THOSE THAT BORE MY MARK...
KILL ME...
THUMP
THUMP
THEY WERE SUCKED INTO THE STORY WORLD, TOO.

FAIRY TALE BATTLE ROYALE

FAIRY TALE BATTLE ROYALE

Chapter 16: Farewell
Costumes

THEY WERE SUCKED INTO THE STORY WORLD ONE HUNDRED YEARS AGO.

ALL OF THE PEOPLE I'VE KILLED SO FAR...

HAVE BEEN...

...
I...

IF THAT'S TRUE...
THEN...

I KNOW THE WEBMASTER OF THE STORY WORLD WEBPAGE.
HOW CAN YOU DO THAT?
"EVERY-ONE" ...?

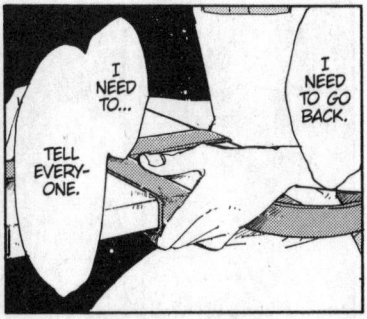
I NEED TO GO BACK.
I NEED TO...
TELL EVERY-ONE.

I NEED TO TELL HIM THE TRUTH.
I HAVE TO STOP EVERYONE FROM KILLING THEIR MAIN CAST...
AND MAKE SURE NO ONE ELSE GETS INVOLVED.

WILL THAT STOP THIS?

WITH RED RIDING HOOD.

I'LL STAY HERE...

WHERE ARE YOU FROM?
I'M...
FROM RUSSIA, ORIGINALLY.
CLINK
CLUNK
RUSSIA.
GLOW
AH, LIKE ME!
...
...
FUKUSHIGE-SAN... ISN'T ANSWERING...
Call
CALL IN PROGRESS
AT THIS RATE, MORE OF THEM WILL...

HURRY ...
I HAVE TO TELL THE OTHERS ...
CREAK
RATTLE
RATTLE ...
BIIING
BOOONG
LET'S GO TO THE ROOF, SHALL WE?
POFF

SO, WE WEREN'T THE ONLY ONES INVOLVED AFTER ALL, HUH?
IT ALL MAKES SENSE NOW...

THIS WILL BE MORE DIFFICULT THAN I THOUGHT.

I HAVE TO TELL HIM.
DON'T.
ALL THE PROTAGONISTS THAT READ HIS PAGE WILL KNOW--

DO YOU KNOW ABOUT THE PROTAGONIST WEBPAGE?
I DO.
IT'S A LOAD OF BULL, RIGHT?
I'VE TALKED TO THE MAN WHO RUNS THE SITE.
OH?

BUT I'M IN THE SAME BOAT AS YOU, KUNINAKA.
I WAS SURPRISED TO SEE YOUR MARK ON SEGAWA AND THE OTHERS.

IT'S JUST GONNA ADD MORE CONFUSION.
BUT THEN PEOPLE WILL KEEP...!

PAT
STILL ...
THERE MUST BE...
!
!...
1-B
IT'S ONE THING TO LET THE OTHER PROTAGONISTS KNOW.
BUT WHAT ABOUT THE FOLKS THAT ALREADY BEAR YOUR MARK?
HOW WILL YOU EXPLAIN THIS?
BUT, YOU KNOW...
PEOPLE HAVE LESS HOPE THAN YOU THINK.
AND STRANGERS EVEN MORESO.
SO, YOU SHOULD THINK OF YOURSELF FOR A WHILE.
THINK... OF GOALS THAT YOU CAN REACH YOURSELF.
YOU'VE HUNG IN THERE.
THAT'S REALLY SOMETHING.

I'M SORRY I COULDN'T HELP.
GO HOME, KUNINAKA.
AND I WILL, TOO.
THUD
YOU DON'T HAVE MUCH TIME LEFT.
HOW DID THINGS...
GET LIKE THIS...?
ALICE

IF ONE PERSON ...
COULD HAVE SEEN...
MY STORY-BOOK...
"REJECT-ED!!"
HA HA HA!

AOBA?

DID YOU GO TO SCHOOL ?
AND SEE YOUR TEACHER ?

I'M HOME.
SO, TELL ME...

BIG SISTER ...
AFTER ALL, WE HAVE PLENTY OF TIME.
WHEN YOU WANT TO TALK, YOU WILL.
YOU'RE NOT GOING TO ASK WHAT'S GOING ON?

WILL YOU COME WITH ME?
I...
I HAVE SOMETHING TO TALK TO MOM AND DAD ABOUT.

HUH?!
RATTLE...
KAWADA

IT'S BEEN A LONG WEEK. IT'S OKAY TO KNOCK OFF EARLY.
...
IS THAT SO?

HONEY, IS EVERY-THING OKAY? IT'S SO EARLY.
ARE YOU SICK?
NO, I'M FINE.

OH, SAYURI JOINED A CLUB...?

ARE THE KIDS HOME?
KENJI'S AT THE POOL...
MIMI'S AT HER ENGLISH SCHOOL ...
AND SAYURI'S AT HER CLUB!

SHE WAS JUST IN THE HOSPITAL.
HOW COULD I NOT WORRY?

"PLEASE DON'T TELL DAD! HE'LL JUST WORRY!"
THAT'S WHAT SHE SAID.
SO I WAS THE ONLY ONE STILL IN THE DARK?

IT'S A MIRACLE.

SHE'S PERKED UP SO FAST.

SHE WAS IN THE HOSPITAL FOR SO LONG...
I GOT USED TO THE WAY SHE WAS IN THERE.
BUT HER ATTITUDE HAS CHANGED SO SUDDENLY.
WITH ME...?
YOU'RE JOKING.
SHE WANTS TO GO TO AN AMUSEMENT PARK.
WELL, IF SHE CAN DO CLUB ACTIVITIES...
THEN WE SHOULD LET HER GO WITH HER FRIENDS.
NO, SHE WANTS TO GO WITH YOU.
SHE'S NOT ACTING OUT.
IT'S JUST THAT SHE CAN FINALLY SHINE.
Going to an Amusement Park with Your Family
HOW ABOUT IT?
LET'S GO ON SUNDAY.

PROTECT OUR CHIL-DREN.
I WANT TO...
I HAVE SOME-THING...
TO TELL YOU.

大学病院
University Hospital

THAT'S JUST SO TYPICAL OF THEM!
OF COURSE THEY DID!
THEY CAME TO PARENT-TEACHER DAY.
OH, FOR THE LOVE OF...!
A MONTH AGO, MAYBE?
WHEN DID MOM AND DAD COME BACK?
UM...

WHERE ARE THE KUNINAKA DOCTORS?
UNFORTUNATELY, THEY'RE PERFORMING A PHYSICAL EXAM.
COULD YOU TELL THEM WE'RE HERE?
PARDON ME, BUT YOU ARE...? DO YOU HAVE AN APPOINTMENT?

GO SIT DOWN ...
I'LL MAKE SURE THEY COME.
OKAY!

I'M KUNINAKA WAKABA.
COULD YOU PLEASE INFORM THEM THAT THEIR *DAUGHTERS* ARE HERE?
Y-YES!

WHICH MEANS HURTING HER FAMILY AND FRIENDS.
BUT...
TO GET RID OF THE IVY, SHE'LL HAVE TO GO AFTER HER MAIN CAST...

AND KATJA DOESN'T HAVE MUCH TIME.
I CAN'T LEAVE RED RIDING HOOD ALONE...
AFTER WE TALK, I HAVE TO GO BACK.

BUT TO MAKE SURE...
NO ONE ELSE SUFFERS...

...!

I'VE SEEN...
THAT MARK BEFORE!

ビク!!
JOLT
AH!
YOUR AUNTS AREN'T HERE YET?
I'LL GO TO THE STORE.
I HAD NO CHOICE.
THEY DON'T SELL FLIP PHONES ANY-MORE...
PEEK
HERE'S YOUR NEW PHONE.
RIGHT OUT OF THE BOX.
I DON'T KNOW HOW IT WORKS.
202

OH ...
HOW STRANGE.

WHAT'S WRONG?
ARE YOU LOST?
AH...
I... UM...

HM?

WOULD YOU LIKE ME TO SHOW YOU TO RECEPTION?
I WAS ALWAYS GETTING LOST IN HERE AT FIRST.
CLACK

TAKUMI HAS A FRIEND THAT'S STILL IN HIGH SCHOOL?
THAT'S UNUSUAL FOR HIM.

HEY, TAKUMI ...
COME OVER HERE.
STOP STARING.
YOU...

WHAT?!
URASHIMA TAROU-SAN?!
I'M...
GONNA GO GET SOME AIR.

YEP.
MY PARENTS WORK HERE.

HAVE YOU... BEEN IN THE HOSPITAL ?

CLACK
CLACK

DO YOU KNOW THE KUNI-NAKA DOCTORS ?

DID YOU MAKE ANY PROGRESS?
AH...
UM...
A LITTLE.
?
AFTER THAT...
I DON'T KNOW ANY DOCTORS' NAMES.
I ONLY WOKE UP RECENTLY.
...
"GOODBYE"?
I CAME HERE TO SAY GOODBYE TO MY PARENTS.
THIS PLACE IS PRETTY CHILL, HUH?
...

TO BE HONEST ...
YOU.
WHERE WERE YOU?!
TAKUMI!
YOU KNOW A LOT ABOUT FAIRY TALES, DON'T YOU?
HM?
UM...
I MEAN...
IN MY OWN WAY...
I SUPPOSE.
WELL, I DON'T.
O...
OH...!
UM ...?!

AND ONCE I LEARNED HOW TO USE AN ITEM FROM THE STORY WORLD...
I GRABBED ANYTHING THAT CAUGHT MY EYE.

PAN-DORA'S BOX.
I SAW IT...

BUT I DIDN'T UNDERSTAND WHEN TO USE THEM.
I DIDN'T HAVE THE TIME TO LOOK THEM UP.

.....
SOMETHING THAT GRANTS WISHES.

LOOKING FOR SOME-THING IN PARTICU-LAR?
ARE YOU...

YOU SHOULD TAKE A LOOK AT WHAT I FOUND.

MY WISH IS...
TO REGAIN THE TIME I WASTED.
SOME-THING THAT WILL UNDO MY CONTRACT.

FAIRY TALE BATTLE ROYALE

Chapter 17: Contact
I saw them from an Area with a large mountain, in a nearby Area with a facade.
Can we meet up to talk about it?
Subject: Definitely!
I look forward to talking with you!
How about you meet me at the Central Station Cafe tomorrow at 10AM?
Subject: RE: Definitely!
Understood.
I look forward to meeting with you.
TAP
TAP
TAP
TAP
I'll be there soon!

CLANG
CLANG
WELCOME~!

GUESS THEY'RE NOT HERE YET.

HMM...
SIT ANY-WHERE YOU'D LIKE!

ONE CUP OF BLENDED COFFEE AND A SAND-WICH.
IT'S...
HIM.
I'm the one wearing the Momorin shirt☆ Look forward to seeing you.

MOMO.
HM?
AHA.

TURN
OH.
THAT WAS QUICK!

YOU MUST BE FUKUSHIGE-SAN.
WE'VE BEEN EXCHANGING EMAILS.
I'M MOMOSE.
Police Officer
Momose Keisuke
SO YOU'RE A COP?
WHAT A SHOCK.
WHAT GREAT SERV--

CLACK
WE'RE NOT HERE TO QUESTION YOU.
PLEASE BE ASSURED OF THAT.
SO, WHY DIDN'T YOU TELL ME?
IT'S NOT LIKE I DID ANYTHING WR--
HE REALLY SHOWED ME HIS BADGE.
ACTUALLY, I WORK IN TRAFFIC.
UM...
...
HAVE YOU DONE SOMETHING WRONG?
BUT SHOULD WE?
YOU JUST SCARED ME.
NO! NOT AT ALL!
AND CORN SOUP!
OKAY, SO ONE BLENDED COFFEE, ONE SANDWICH...
COMING RIGHT UP!
RUMBLE
AND I'LL HAVE SOME CHOCOLATE CAKE.
OKAY!
I'LL HAVE A HAMBURGER.

I ALWAYS THOUGHT THAT JAPANESE BURGERS WERE A BIT SMALL...
BUT THIS ONE IS GREAT! IT'S HUGE!
YOUR JAPANESE IS GOOD.
ARE YOU A COP, TOO?
YES.

OH, THAT'S RIGHT. I HAVEN'T INTRODUCED MYSELF.
I'M A DETECTIVE FROM AMERICA.
YOU CAN CALL ME CAMILLA.

WE DON'T HAVE A LOT OF TIME.
PLEASE TRY TO RELAX.
WE'VE COME TO AID YOUR EFFORTS, FUKUSHIGE-SAN.
WELL, THAT TAKES A LOAD OFF MY SHOULDERS.

SO, MOMOSE-SAN FROM TRAFFIC...
ARE YOU A PROTAGONIST, TOO?
I SEE.

DO YOU HAVE INFORMATION ON THE PERSON I'M LOOKING FOR?
BECAUSE I'M GETTING NOWHERE.
BUT IF THE POLICE ARE GONNA HELP ME, I'LL EXPECT A LOT~!

WELL, WE DID BROACH THE SUBJECT IN OUR EMAIL.
WE HAVE AN AREA THAT HAS NO IDENTIFYING CHARACTERISTICS. A *TABULA RASA*, OF SORTS...
THAT'S WHERE WE MET THEM.
AH...
DID YOU TALK TO THEM?
NO.
WE DIDN'T.
NOT REALLY.

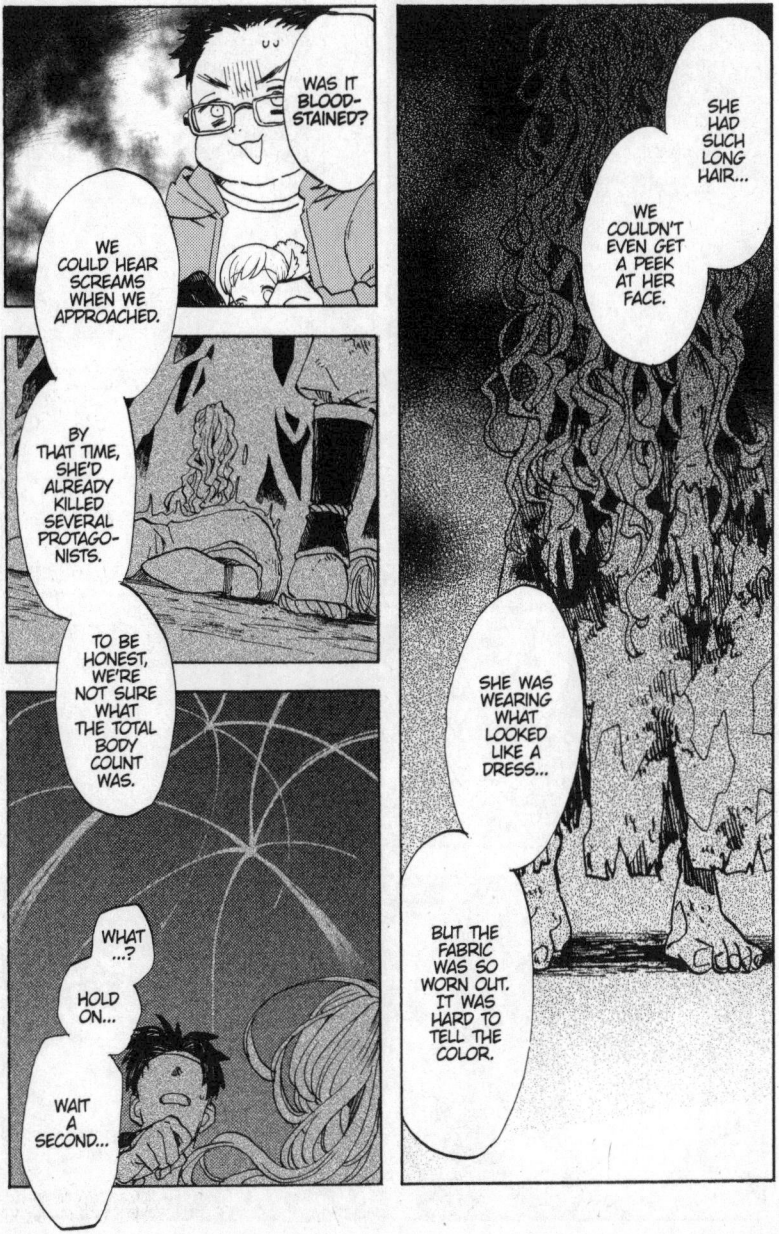
WAS IT BLOOD-STAINED?
WE COULD HEAR SCREAMS WHEN WE APPROACHED.
BY THAT TIME, SHE'D ALREADY KILLED SEVERAL PROTAGO-NISTS.
TO BE HONEST, WE'RE NOT SURE WHAT THE TOTAL BODY COUNT WAS.
WHAT ...?
HOLD ON...
WAIT A SECOND...
SHE HAD SUCH LONG HAIR...
WE COULDN'T EVEN GET A PEEK AT HER FACE.
SHE WAS WEARING WHAT LOOKED LIKE A DRESS...
BUT THE FABRIC WAS SO WORN OUT. IT WAS HARD TO TELL THE COLOR.

ge!
ACCORD-ING TO YOUR SITE, SHE CAN CHANGE INTO A WOLF, RIGHT?
Monika Raion
Wanted list for: "The Werewolf's Daughter"
Can shift shape from human to wolf form
Color in the story world: Grey
Tall
Help us find this pe
Schange!
BUT NO ONE SAID SHE WAS SO DANGEROUS!
IT'S PRETTY CLOSE TO WHAT I POSTED...
THAT SOUNDS LIKE THE PERSON I'M LOOKING FOR!
IT WAS ONLY FOR A SECOND...
BUT WHAT WE THOUGHT WAS A WOMAN CHANGED INTO A WOLF.
SHE NEARLY BIT MY HEAD OFF.

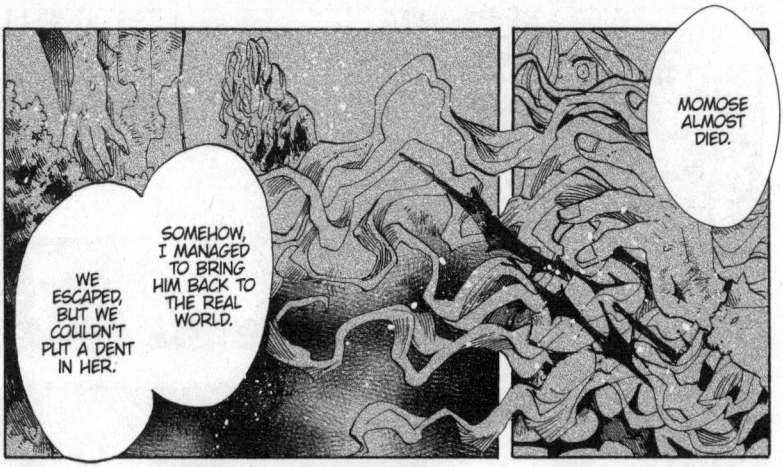
MOMOSE ALMOST DIED.
SOMEHOW, I MANAGED TO BRING HIM BACK TO THE REAL WORLD.
WE ESCAPED, BUT WE COULDN'T PUT A DENT IN HER.

AFTER THAT, WE TRIED TO FIND OUT MORE.
AND THAT'S WHEN WE FOUND YOUR WEBPAGE.
WHY ARE YOU LOOKING FOR HER?
IT SOUNDED LIKE SOMEONE HAD ASKED YOU TO FIND HER, YES?
AND IF THAT'S THE CASE...

COULD YOU TELL US...
WHO ASKED YOU TO LOOK?
OH CRAP...

HOW DID THE PREVIOUS RED RIDING HOOD MANAGE TO SURVIVE ALL THIS TIME?
I WAS PLANNING TO TRADE INFO ON THE WEREWOLF'S DAUGHTER FOR ANSWERS, BUT NOW...
EVEN THOUGH THERE'S NO SET MAXIMUM NUMBER OF SURVIVORS, I STILL DON'T REALLY WANT TO TELL THESE PEOPLE THAT ARE OVERFLOWING WITH SUCH A...
HEALTHY SENSE OF JUSTICE.
I...
NEED SOME TIME.
SHE'S OUT THERE TARGETING PEOPLE AS WE SPEAK.
AGREED. THAT'S NOT REASONABLE.
WE CAN'T LET HER HURT ANYONE ELSE.
WE HAVE TO STOP HER NOW.

Reach
LET'S TEAM UP.
FELLOW PROTAGO-NISTS.

WE CAN SAVE THEM.

WE HAVE TO ACT.

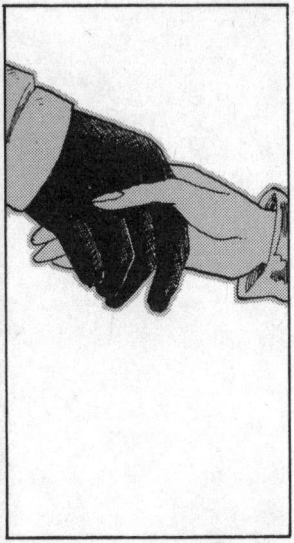

Volume ④ : END

FAIRY TALE BATTLE ROYALE

Character
Name:
Shimamoto Takumi
Age: 24
Interests: Maintaining his motorcycle
Special Skill: Maintaining his motorcycle
Family: Father, mother, grandmother
Contracted Fairy Tale:
"Urashima Tarou"

character
Name:
Kawada Shougo
Age: 33
Interests: Mountain climbing
Special Skill:
Kindling fires
Family: Wife, two daughters, one son
Contracted Fairy Tale:
"The White Snake"
(The Brothers Grimm)

FAIRY TALE BATTLE ROYALE

I THINK THIS IS WHERE AOBA FOUND THE TEA LEAVES...
THUNK

I'M GONNA GO MAKE MORE TEA OKAY?
I'VE CAUSED SO MUCH TROUBLE...
I SHOULD MAKE IT UP TO HER.

After Aoba returned to the real world.
IT'S PROBABLY COLD BY NOW.
THE TEA...

GUG
GUG
rumble
rumble
rumble...
Thud
RATTLE
RUMBLE
RUMBLE
RUMBLE

CLANG...

SHE WAS SO CLUMSY THAT THE NOISE...
ATTRACTED A GAGGLE OF MUMMIES.

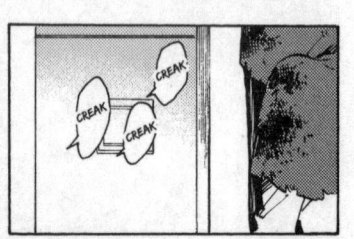
CREAK
CREAK
CREAK

wobble
I MADE TEA!
ALL RIGHT.
...

I THINK THIS IS WHERE AOBA FOUND THE TEA LEAVES...
THUNK

I'M GONNA GO MAKE MORE TEA, OKAY?
I'VE CAUSED SO MUCH TROUBLE...
I SHOULD MAKE IT UP TO HER.

After Aoba returned to the real world.
THE TEA...
IT'S PROBABLY COLD BY NOW.

rumble
rumble
rumble...
GUG
GUG
Thud
RATTLE
RUMBLE
RUMBLE
RUMBLE

CLANG...

ATTRACTED A GAGGLE OF MUMMIES.
SHE WAS SO CLUMSY THAT THE NOISE...

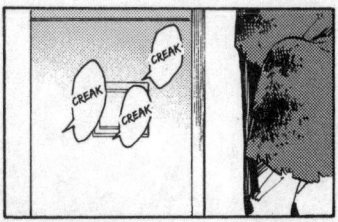
CREAK
CREAK
CREAK

wobble
I MADE TEA!
ALL RIGHT.
...

FAIRY
TALE
BATTLE
ROYALE